AND YET

poems by

Rita Coleman

Finishing Line Press
Georgetown, Kentucky

AND YET

Copyright © 2017 by Rita Coleman
ISBN 978-1-63534-290-1 First Edition
All rights reserved under International and Pan-American Copyright Conventions. No part of this book may be reproduced in any manner whatsoever without written permission from the publisher, except in the case of brief quotations embodied in critical articles and reviews.

ACKNOWLEDGMENTS

The author gratefully acknowledges Pauletta Hansel and fellow poets who have provided feedback in the crafting of these poems, and to the editors of the following publications in which the ensuing poems have appeared, some in earlier versions.

"And Yet," "Creek Talk," "In Praise of Children Who Don't Listen," "The Trees"—*From the Tower*
"Ending, Beginning," "I Dreamed of A Condor, Peacock-Hued"—*The Way the Light Slants*
"Narcissus" (Titled "Alternate Reality")—*Poppy Road Review*
"O'Bannon Creek Speaks"—*The Way the Light Slants* and *From the Tower*
"Unseen Bodhisattvas"—*Sangha in Motion*
"Where Air Grows"—*Common Threads*

Publisher: Leah Maines

Editor: Christen Kincaid

Cover Art: Rita Coleman

Author Photo: Frank Baxley

Cover Design: Elizabeth Maines McCleavy

Printed in the USA on acid-free paper.
Order online: www.finishinglinepress.com
also available on amazon.com

Author inquiries and mail orders:
Finishing Line Press
P. O. Box 1626
Georgetown, Kentucky 40324
U. S. A.

Table of Contents

Where Air Grows 1
Light Year 2
In Praise of Children Who Don't Listen 3
The Ultimate Impressionist Wing 4
Symmetry: A Painterly Ideal 5
Narcissus 6
Unseen Bodhisattvas 7
This Fabric Called Grandmother 8
Creek Talk 9
Ending, Beginning 10
Just Shifted 11
Of What Do We Make Our Poetry? 12
Drought 13
O'Bannon Creek Speaks 15
A Catfish Day 16
The Trees 17
A Lesson in Love 18
I Dreamed of a Condor, Peacock-Hued 19
Wounded Heart 20
Tarot Card #8 21
And Yet 22
Questions and Answer 23

Where Air Grows

I carefully uproot prickly thistle,
bedstraw, anonymous weeds,
from a bed of leggy iris, lavender and yellow

Opening their world to space between
where air grows, where thoughts
become things, ideas, sweat.

Above nodding blossoms, white cotton
café curtains frame another space.
In there, day begins, a plumped pillow

Willing to support heavy thoughts
that refract in lead crystal,
small rainbows, tiny prisms

That, unchecked, become tiny prisons.
The key, beside the pillow now
lumpy and flat, is golden.

Light Year

Time chases the sun across fields shorn for harvest,
the moon into darkness, the tides into full and least,
days shadowed into yesterday.

Holographs, relative, transitory, shimmer-light,
minutes tock into nothingness
while hours crawl, sluggards that they are,

Or race into tomorrow, head-spinning.
Ride the wave, smooth as the ocean,
or jounce on the wild-haired particle.

Notice the standstill of the past, the fuzzy future,
the moving sidewalk on which you place your life today.
While you live on the bridge spanning the earth and sun,

Take a chance. Dive in the light year, swim in the swirl
as it widens, narrows, mesmerizes, mystifies,
taking you deeper and deeper into the light.

In Praise of Children Who Don't Listen

When asked why, they say *Sometimes I don't want to listen.*
Fair enough you think.
You remember what it's like
Filling every waffle hole with syrup
Pondering the swirling bathtub drain
Feathertouching a cicada shell, brown, brittle, cramped
Gazing out of focus, losing what self you have in dreaminess
while people taller and older interrupt your world.

But you say *I need you to listen*
Because saying it twice or even three times demands
more words for your tired mouth.
That squirrel could bite
No running on the couch
That is not *stable*
Over and over day after day, alert, you repeat
because your job is to keep little bodies safe.

Yet you long to uphold the right to not listen,
to silence those damnable interruptions for
A glint off a golden dome
A mockingbird's tumblesong
A green bite of parsley from the earth
Sensations, colors, shapes, gaining admittance—or not.
Now that you're older you can. But do you?
Or do the conspirators have all your attention?

The Ultimate Impressionist Wing
Water Lilies, Claude Monet, Oils; The Starry Night,
Vincent van Gogh, Oils; The Dancers, Edgar Degas, Oils;
Luncheon of the Boating Party, Auguste Renoir, Oils; Margot
and Her Mother Seated on a Sofa, Mary Cassatt, Drypoint

The Mistral Wind sweeps paintings out of their frames,
Monet's water lilies whirling like animated fairies.

Van Gogh's spiral sun spins into the sky,
secure as if it had always been hung there.

Degas' ballet dancers hip-hop to a boom-box,
toss pointe shoes out the window.

Renoir's gazing maiden takes her swain's hand,
leads him off the boat at the next pier.

Cassatt's Margot and her mother belly-laugh
so hard a weak leg of the sofa gives way.

And it goes on: Manets, Sisleys, Pissarros, Cezannes, Gaugins . . .

Paintings step beyond oils and linseed, board and canvas,
beyond time and dimensions; they invite you to come along.

You follow with no questions, assured you are safe.
Even if your life is spinning out of control, you're happy.

Symmetry: A Painterly Ideal

An idea, rather than two mirrored halves
a kind of pleasing equality,
a balance of unsprung chaos
with one bold blast
devolves into anarchy.
Entropy reigns,
inertia collapses.
A great kinesis marches
cobalts, cadmiums, ultramarines—
swirls and points and dabs and swashes—
out of the frame.
They gallop, squeal,
slide, skate, swing,
saunter, waltz,
gyrate, twist, turn,
flow, fly,
and wing into the distance
chirping, tweeting, honking,
farewell.

Narcissus

If Narcissus the god had gazed at the narcissus flower
blooming somewhere in the folds of the earth,
If he had become enchanted by the warm yellow center,
enticed by slender, waving, come-hither lovelies,
entered the tubal opening, finding mirrored passion,
he would have beheld beauty staring back at him,
rather than the shallow reflection of his face in a pond,
a reflection, that had a wind arisen, would have blurred,
been erased.

Unseen Bodhisattvas

uninterested in nirvana,
sit on porch swings, rocking, swaying.

Gauzy, round, webbed,
a dream catcher woven with purpose,
interpreting visions, bestowing the best.

Still, sculpted, a morning rabbit,
brown eyes glistening, its only hint
of hidden, ocular humor.

Hushed zephyr, subtle, drifting onto
bare arms, vulnerable to the cross-breeze
that wafts, shifts.

Unseen bohdisattvas, their capacity for enlightenment
requires no form, no shape, no size, no heartbeat.
A handsel for amazement is the genius.

This Fabric Called Grandmother

*In radiant moonlight the Ancient One
weaves on the age-old loom
this fabric called* Grandmother.

Woven inside her, thread after thread of
first moments and amazing lives,

Threads the color of wildness and intensity,
love, pastel and bold,

The smooth laying down of face and soul,
the deep weave of length and breadth,

A rhythm unpatterned, random and perfect,
not yet done, a continuous beyond.

Creek Talk

The noiseless steps of my shoes on a path ridged
with roots, mounded with rocks, angled, uneven, soft-sloped

Quiet enough for the changeling mockingbird to continue
its repertoire in the leafless walnut.

My dad was a silent walker, outdoors
and indoors where he soft-shut doors and drawers.

I was sure it was the Cherokee in us,
my great-grandmother like so many others claimed.

In the drape of smoky mountains and rock-hopping rivers,
all nature-bound events, I live like she did.

I speak creek-talk. I sense the wild rumble of sky
and earth before it rattles the bones of the living.

My second sight is first sight nestled in the language
of mounded peaks, cold springs, and river rock.

When my eyes glimpse the first ridge as flatland
gives way to the southern rise, I'm certain

That I belong in the cool shadow of a sun-blocked mountain
that still gives birth to spirits who see beyond the horizon.

Ending, Beginning

When the ash wing dove
dips my way
on the day
that is my last,
I will float
onto its feathered back
lean low
steady, ready
to soar into
the near unseen
a teardrop
in someone's eye
a sigh
in someone's breath
an ache
in someone's chest.

As the ash wing dove
flies closer
to the sweet place,
lands from memory
on the unmarked space,
ascends to the far world again—
a distant place nearly forgotten—
my voice
drops away
my eyes
settle deep inside me
my body
is a flash of gold.

Just Shifted

Cry as many tears as you need
but don't make sorrow your life.

Miss me, yes, in the space
beside you, now empty.

Know this rounded earth holds
my shrouded bones.

Twilight suggests
my shadowed face,

My whispers speak
in the sureness of your heart.

When your joy returns,
different, yet real,

Song sparrows will
trill you awake in spring

Heady French lilac
will envelope you,

My voice will sing in your laughter
speak in your caution.

I will not be erased–
just shifted.

Of What Do We Make Our Poetry?

Is it the thrum of a ruby-throat,
the hovering of a silver blue damsel fly,
the hushed creek whispering to the river far ahead?

Is it a chilled desert night, no need of a telescope,
the calving of a blue glacier,
the Honduran island with red hibiscus?

Is it the silked cheeks of a little one,
the fluff of a pup,
the velvet of a touch?

Is it the pain of all their last breaths,
harsh words in public places,
holding a pet for the last time?

Is it the original dream of to be,
the large number of years gone, irretrievable,
the ease of longevity?

It is all and none, these and more,
tears and keening, bougainvillea and hot tea,
gazing and surprise, you and me.

Drought

Beyond dry,
this garden of words,
shriveled, crisp,
stunted, weary.

Who knows
when torrents
of words
will rain day after day.

Catch the run-off in a barrel.

Admire glossy leaves
sturdy stems
ripe fruits
plump vegetables
all good nature
sun and shade.

Who knows when the land
will be struck dry
morning dew the only reminder
of what *could* be,
if drops fell from a cloud.

Too hot-tired to water,
fatigue folding into malaise
into bone-sucking ennui.

Words hidden, so far away.

*Scratch the seeds
from the pods,
what you can find.*

*Find the letters.
Find the words.
Find the rain.*

O'Bannon Creek Speaks

Hop on this dimpled disc of water
spinning into a
fan of ripples.
Ride the white caps
round the boulders.
Leave behind the blue belle
and the red flit of the air.
You can fly later.

Look!
Behind you is stillness.
Ahead, an adventure.
Right now I'm here with you.
But hurry.
I'll be gone before you exhale.
Gone, yet here,
another stream of water,
added to, taken away.

At least try.
Crawl in between
these moist layers of limestone
until you're ready to plunge.
Gaze on the shimmer of
a damsel fly hovering above
the surface ready to dive.
Or hang onto the branch like that
water skater, lolling and content,
and rest.

Catfish Day

A low-slung concrete pier, the end scrabbled, pocked,
feet outstretched, seat damp, shoes wet
sun bright, April blue
cumulus drift echoes river's meander
watersounds   a cat lapping at the broken dock
ripple   pause   ripple
spring-bare weeds poking above a dappled surface
water-plop
           frog splash
                      quicker than sight
mid-river, an air bubble–*puhp*–another, another.

Behind, winter's backwash, a once-white sock,
an orange laundry detergent bottle, label washed away,
fitting, these together in stippled mud-quick
left by water rising, receding.

Across, another bank, cut into the hill, the river's doing,
a border of sycamores and maples, green leafed, ready,
distant buzz of a race car, a humming bee, lost on the edge.

Lean into a catfish day soothed by easy green water.

The Trees

are waiting for you.
They've invited you to every party they've ever hosted.
Often you come with spooky stories,
tents that fall down in the night,
marshmallow, chocolate, and graham crackers.
Then you leave, forgetting.

If you know the language of ash, maple, oak,
all the arboreal cousins, you will discover incredibilities:
where Queen Turtle Big Ellen suns on the Little Miami,
why jewelweed and poison ivy grow together,
how we used to sleep in the branches of our home tree,
all of this transmitted by
secrets riding on waves of thoughts
whispers only the West Wind can hear
mysteries in birdsong melodies.

Outrider trees, the tallest, scout for people, deer, bears,
and scurry creatures.
Senior trees tumblespeak caution to the youngers, to be patient,
to not be in such a hurry to grow up.

The next time you hike, drive, swim, glide, float, or fly
past a stand of trees, a forest, a copse, a lone tree,
be ready.
The picture that floats into your mind may be
a tree stump calling out to come have a sit,
one of the dancing trees hiking up its roots for a dosy-doe,
a crooked finger branch, beckoning.

This is your invitation.

Consider stopping.

A Lesson in Love

We should take time for love more often, I say, so we wander
to the outdoor deck. Rather than tiki torches that flicker and wave,
the light of LunaMoon silvers us, silvers the sea.

The great ocean murmur soothes our shell ears,
pounds distant rock face, rises in spray, falls back on itself,
becomes the still of sea glass beyond sight, beyond light.

We are Atlantic, Pacific, Indian, Arctic, Southern,
the rhythm of waves and breath and moods and stars,
sanded stretches and ice-clad mountains.

Our footprints separate starfish and sunrise shells
the pastel of sunrise, the muted cobalt of twilight.
Oceanic will o' the wisps, flicker and flame, beckon

In whispers carried by the susurrus, to plunge
into the joy of deep, penetrating heartsoul, and roll
in the rock of the waves. Bouyed in safety,

Bask in the mirror of LunaLight, ride foaming surf
onto grainy sand, settle amid shags of seaweed,
framed by smooth driftwood bleached nearly white.

You sigh, I sigh. We help each other through the door,
your shiny, wooden cane, my shiny metal walker. You
brush my gray hair off my neck and kiss my tender spot.

I Dream of a Condor, Peacock-Hued

Identified by the wing span
seven feet across,
it flies an incredible
windswept body
toward the temple
not ruined
but ancient
in Peru.

I gawp in awe
as its feathers change
to iridescent greens and
blues, wings taking on
the colors of courtship.
But this condor is
wooing the divine,
the unseen holy.

This sacred mating
deepens in mystery
into aquas and vermilions
until color becomes
unnecessary and
flight a mere tool
to become
the Beloved.

Wounded Heart

Birdling drags a sprained wing
leaving a side-swath in morning grass
sun-sparked with dew.

Fertile bed of primrose awaits,
purple, yellow, crimson,
to heal the bruising.

A splint of poetry
a poultice of love song
a palette of pastels
crystallize.

Wings grow the length of rainbows
sweep particles of light before and after
ride sky light and cloud rims,

Back and forth, back and forth,
brush whispers of cherry, orange, plum,
against the canvas of canopy,

Circling in thermals, no effort,
until a sponge of earth unfolds
as darkening quiets the day.

Bird cocks her head toward
silent music of dusk
and tucks into her wing for sleep.

Tarot Card #8

The sky of lemon sun
cascades as garlands
of dandelions
that drape her long, white, linen dress.

Her hands, one damaged, one healthy,
stroke the shaggy-soft mane
of her lion neighbor,
an old friend from childhood.

While her feet root in solid earth,
she saunters, a golden gladiolia,
tall energy soothing the realm,
with light-filled hands,
the damaged the most brilliant.

Soothing murmurs from her lips
waft on the fragrance of summer,
a kaleidoscope of colors
on a palette of green.

Distant peaks, white-topped
and hazed by a blue horizon,
invite her to stay in this reality
a sacred community
where damaged healers thrive.

And Yet

Out of the inky spill
emerge tiny objects
sculpted into
faces, words, wings.
Drumbeats coax
them into villages
of shadows.

The search for sky virtues
designed only for the earth—
caves, fields, rivers—
leads to dwellings of
long-ago mothers
and terrified children
vigilant for night monsters.

Starborn birds
drop feathers of hope
scarlet
azure
iridescent
reassuring lost ones
they will find the way.

When forgiveness is served
knots of fury untangle,
woven love
cradles earthen plates
and primitive paintings
lit by a circle of firebright,
all of it fragrant as star anise.

Questions and Answer
>From multimedia art *Four Directions*
by Gary Gaffney

Is it the hand of God,
if God has a hand,
if there is that kind of god,
that points to our galaxy home?

Aren't we just a tribe of stars
flying, slithering, galloping, clawing,
sloshing, walking, chakra-ed, and wide-eyed
breathing ribboned air in the blue of knowing?

No need for the North Star, right here.
No sky map, no star chart. We are certain
where to begin and when to end,
grand, humble lights, vast vista of seamless being.

Rita Coleman writes award-winning poetry, memoir, and picture books in rural Greene County, Ohio. A former journalist and educator, her work has been published in anthologies and literary journals. Rita's first poetry chapbook, *Mystic Connections*, 2009, is described by *Kirkus* as "deeply felt." Her attendance at writing workshops includes the University of Iowa, Antioch Writers Workshop, and Thomas More College as well as state and national workshops with SCBWI (the Society for Children's Book Writers and Illlustrators). Rita reads her poetry on *Conrad's Corner* WYSO 91.3 FM along with other regional poets.

She holds a BA and an MA in English Literature, with a Concentration in Creative Writing, from Wright State University, Dayton, Ohio. She has been a poetry/memoir student of Pauletta Hansel, the first Poet Laureate of Cincinnati, since 2013.

Rita is a talented photographer and has been a member of Town and Country Fine Arts Gallery and the Dayton Visual Art Center. Her photos are exhibited in juried art shows and regional venues.

Rita is married and lives in a restored farmhouse with her husband Frank Baxley and their cat EL BK, fractured Spanglish for The Black Kitty.

Visit her website www.ritacoleman.com

www.ingramcontent.com/pod-product-compliance
Lightning Source LLC
LaVergne TN
LVHW041521070426
835507LV00012B/1729